Black's Sketchbooks

London · Adam & Charles Black

1 London
2 Edinburgh
3 Cambridge
4 Stratford on Avon
5 Bath and Wells
6 Canterbury

PUBLISHED BY
A. & C. BLACK · SOHO SQUARE · LONDON W.

CAMBRIDGE

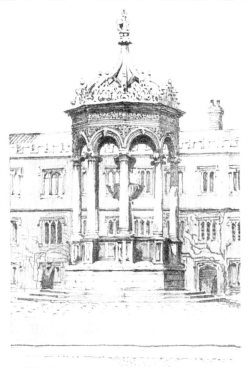

A SKETCH-BOOK BY
WALTER M. KEESEY.

A & C. BLACK, LTD.
SOHO SQUARE, LONDON.

Drawings

1 The Fountain, Trinity College (Title Page)
2 Clare Gates and King's College Chapel
3 Clare Bridge
4 King's College Chapel – West End
5 St. John's College Gateway
6 Old Bridge, St. John's College
7 Great Court, Trinity College
8 The Master's Lodge, Downing College
9 New Court, Sidney Sussex College
10 The Round Church
11 Cloister Court, Queen's College
12 The President's Garden, Queen's College
13 Market Day
14 Trumpington Street
15 Northampton Street

CLARE GATE &
KING'S CHAPEL.

CLARE BRIDGE
OVER BANKS.

KING'S CHAPEL.

JOHN'S COLLEGE
GATEWAY ≡

JOHNS GATEWAY
TO BACKS.

TRINITY COLLEGE
FOUNTAIN COURT.

MASTER'S LODGE
DOWNING COLLEGE.

SIDNEY SUSSEX COLLEGE. NEW COURT.

QUEEN'S CLOISTER
COURT.

QUEEN'S COLL.
MAKER'S GARDEN

TRUMPINGTON STREET.

NORTHAMPTON STREET
CORNER

First published in Great Britain in 1913
by A&C Black Publishers
36 Soho Square
London W1D 3QY
www.acblack.com

This edition published 2009

© 1913, 2009 A&C Black

ISBN 978-14081-1123-9

A CIP record of this book is available from the British Library

Printed and bound in China